Grace Hopper

The First Woman to
Program the First Computer
in the United States

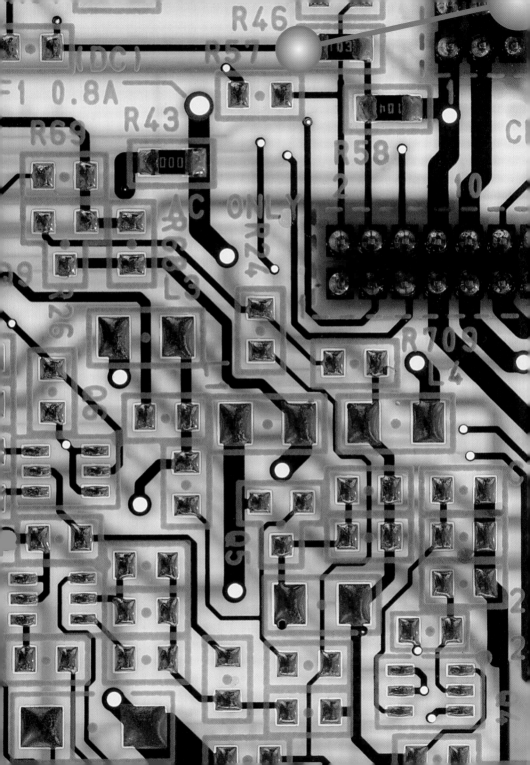

Women Hall of Famers in
Mathematics and Science

Grace Hopper

The First Woman to
Program the First Computer
in the United States

Christy Marx

the rosen publishing group's
**rosen
central**

Dedicated with love to my parents: to my mother for the gift of dreams, and to my father for the gift of reason

I'd like to give special thanks to Ellen Guon Beeman, Stephen Beeman, and Karen Williams for proofreading and helping me get the technical details right, and to Dr. Peggy Aldrich Kidwell for sharing her time and expertise.

Published in 2004 by The Rosen Publishing Group, Inc.
29 East 21st Street, New York, NY 10010

Library of Congress Cataloging-in-Publication Data

Marx, Christy.
Grace hopper : the first woman to program the first computer in the united states / By Christy Marx.— 1st ed.
    p. cm. — (Women hall of famers in mathematics and science)
Includes bibliographical references and index.
ISBN 0-8239-3877-8
1. Hopper, Grace Murray. 2. Women computer engineers—United States—Biography. 3. Electronic data processing—Biography. I. Title. II. Series.
QA76.2.H67 M37 2002   JB
305.43'6213—dc21   HOPPER, G.
                c.)   2002009414

Manufactured in the United States of America

Contents

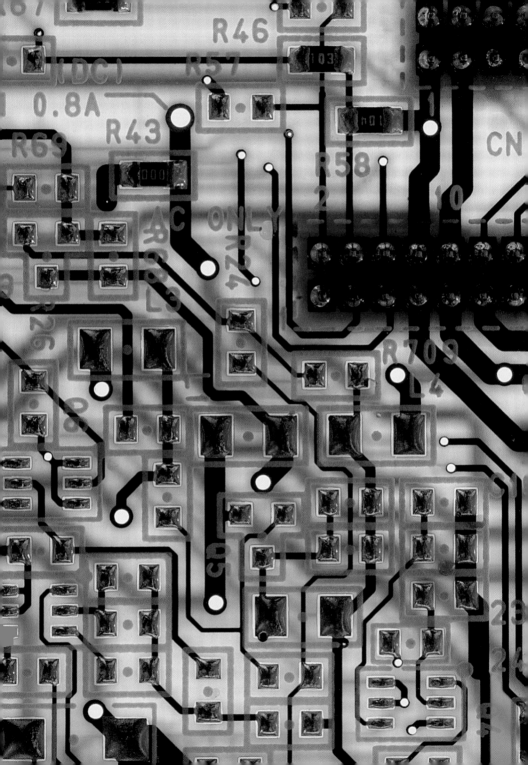

Introduction

Grace Hopper was known as "Amazing Grace," the "Grand Old Lady of Software," the "First Lady" of data processing, the "Mother of Modern Naval Computing," and "Grandma COBOL."

She was utterly dedicated to the service of her country and served in the U.S. Navy for forty-three years, rising to the high rank of rear admiral. She was a mathematical genius at a time when women weren't even expected to go to college, achieving honors and degrees that only a few other women of her time managed to accomplish. She was instrumental in developing many of the vital procedures that have made modern computers possible. In this field she has a long string of firsts and unusual accomplishments, from being the first woman to program the first computer in the United States to being the first woman and sometimes the first American to win certain national and international honors.

Grace Hopper was a tireless advocate of innovative thinking, finding new and better ways to get things done and bucking the system. She never let anything stand in her way, and she overcame obstacles of gender and age, not once but many times. She even faced the unusual hurdles of being considered too short and too thin!

She was truly "Amazing Grace."

1

The Tomboy Years

Grace Hopper was born Grace Brewster Murray on December 9, 1906. To get a sense of how dramatically things would change during her lifetime, imagine this: There were no mass-produced cars when Grace was born. Orville Wright had made the first test flight of an airplane only three years before. There was no television, and silent movies had been around for only a couple of years. There were no home refrigerators or frozen foods. No world war had been fought yet. And, of course, computers had not yet been invented.

Grace's childhood was spent in New York City. The corner of Fifth Avenue and Forty-second Street looked much different in the early 1900s than it does today. People dressed in formal clothing that was much different from what people currently wear, and horse-drawn carriages were the preferred means of transportation.

THE EARLY YEARS

Grace was born in New York City. Her mother, Mary Campbell Van Horne Murray, named Grace after her best friend, Grace Brewster. Mary had a deep interest in mathematics and studied geometry, but when she was a young girl, it wasn't considered proper for a young lady to study math. Her love of math was clearly passed on to her first daughter.

Grace was the oldest of her siblings. Her younger sister, Mary, was three years younger than Grace. Her brother, Roger, was five years younger. Grace's father, Walter Fletcher Murray, was an insurance broker and came from a line of builders and engineers. Walter suffered from hardening of the arteries during a time when medical treatment couldn't do much for him. When Grace entered high school, her father had to have both of his legs amputated. In spite of this, he lived to be seventy-five, getting around on wooden legs with the help of canes. He was an inspirational man who never let himself be stopped by adversity. This courage was passed on to his children.

EQUAL OPPORTUNITY PARENTING

Walter Murray was also unusual for a man of his time because he believed his daughters should have the same educational opportunities as his son, and he wanted them to spend a year working before they went to college so they would have skills with which to support themselves. With this kind of supportive family, it's no wonder Grace had the will to learn and succeed at whatever she did.

Grace was an adventurous girl who liked to climb trees, play cops and robbers, and play a game called kick-the-can. She had nontraditional toys such as construction sets and building blocks. All of the children, including Roger, were taught practical skills such as sewing, gardening, and cooking. However, Grace also learned to knit, crochet, do needlepoint, and play the piano. She loved to read, and one of her favorite books was Rudyard Kipling's *Just So Stories*.

A NATURAL CURIOSITY

In the summers, the family spent time at their cottage on Lake Wentworth in Wolfeboro, New Hampshire, where Grace always had a wonderful time swimming and sailing. As a child, she was consumed with curiosity about how things worked. Author Charlene Billings had the good fortune to interview Grace Hopper for her book *Grace Hopper: Navy Admiral and Computer Pioneer*, in which Grace said that she could not resist a good gadget. When she was seven years old, Grace took apart an alarm clock to see how it worked, then couldn't figure out how to put it back together. She went around the cottage and took apart six more clocks before her mother caught her. Grace was confined to fiddling around with only one clock after that.

Grace told Charlene Billings the story of a moment with her father that stuck in her memory. One night in 1910, her father showed her Halley's comet. She thought it looked brighter than the Moon. He predicted that she would live to see Halley's comet return in 1986, and she did.

It was common for girls to be sent to private schools at the time. Grace went to Schoonmakers School, a private school in New York City that emphasized reading, history, and basic educational skills. Though girls were supposed to learn how to be ladies, Grace was able to play basketball, field hockey, and water polo. She was physically very small, but she had energy and personality to spare. Being tiny didn't stop her from taking part in sports where her size would have been a disadvantage.

Getting an Education

2

Grace advanced quickly in school. When she was only sixteen, she applied to the prestigious Vassar College in Poughkeepsie, New York. She would have made it in at that time except that she flunked a Latin exam. She didn't like having to speak foreign languages, but she enjoyed reading them.

Vassar College made Grace wait a year before allowing her to join as a student. During that time, Grace stayed at the Hartridge School in Plainfield, New Jersey, as a boarding student. Hartridge School was an all-girls school that taught college preparatory courses. Girls were also expected to take part in singing, dancing, and other forms of exercise, such as gymnastics or calisthenics. Grace played hockey and basketball, worked on the school paper, and acted in the school plays.

She graduated from Hartridge in 1924, ready to begin her college career. Next to her picture in the yearbook was this quotation by William Jennings Bryan: "In action faithful and in honor clear."

EXCELLING AT VASSAR

Vassar College was established in 1861 with the purpose of providing an all-women college that offered the same high educational standards as any all-male school. This was the perfect place for a bold, independent young woman like Grace Murray. She not only took her registered courses but also added courses in all of the sciences, including botany, geology, and physiology, along with courses in economics and business. Grace also pursued studies in mathematics and physics, while keeping up with her sports activities, such as basketball. She was eager to learn and she was a hard worker.

Grace studied at Vassar College, a prestigious school in Poughkeepsie, New York, from 1924 to 1928. While in college, she honed her teaching skills by tutoring her fellow students.

The teachers quickly noticed that Grace had a talent for teaching. She was asked to tutor other students in physics, which allowed her to go beyond talking about theory by doing practical demonstrations. Throughout her career, Grace used practical methods to bridge the gap between theory and reality, and to help her students better understand complicated scientific terms.

Throughout her life, Grace was a woman who excelled in everything she pursued. After graduating with honors from Vassar College, she went on to Yale University, where she earned a master's degree in 1930. Only four years later, she completed her doctoral work at Yale, at that time a rare feat for a woman in mathematics.

She kept her adventurous spirit. Grace remembered one day when a biplane landed near the school. She described what it was like in *Grace Hopper: Navy Admiral and Computer Pioneer*: "Wood, linen, and wire. It had one engine and an open cockpit so you got the full benefit of the wind." Grace decided to blow all the money she had with her—an entire ten dollars—to go up for a ride.

FROM VASSAR TO YALE

In 1928, she graduated from Vassar College with a bachelor of arts degree in mathematics and physics. She was elected to Phi Beta Kappa, which is a very high honor. Phi Beta Kappa is an honor society that selects members on the basis of academic achievement.

Grace also received a grant from Vassar that allowed her to continue her education. Otherwise, she might have gone to work, since she was worried about how her parents could afford sending her sister, Mary, and her brother, Roger, to college in their turns. Mary ended up going to Vassar, and Roger followed his older sister Grace to Yale.

Grace went to Yale University in Connecticut, where she continued her studies. Her roommate at Yale gave her a Boston terrier. Grace had the dog for ten years.

Two years later, in 1930, she received a master's degree in mathematics and physics.

MARRIED LIFE

On June 15, 1930, when she was twenty-three years old, Grace Murray married Vincent Foster Hopper. They were married in the same church in which Grace's parents had been married. In fact,

HONORARY DOCTORATES

During her lifetime, Grace Hopper was awarded at least thirty-seven honorary doctorates. These are special degrees given out by universities to some-one who has shown exceptional merit in his or her field, or accomplished some-thing that is worthy of being honored.

Receiving so many honorary doctorates proves that the con-tributions Dr. Hopper made to math and science were very highly valued indeed.

Grace Hopper receiving an honorary degree from Drexel University in 1987

the same man who had performed the wedding ceremony also performed Grace and Vincent's wedding ceremony!

Vincent Hopper was a highly educated man who graduated with honors from Princeton

University. He taught English and studied comparative literature at Columbia University.

Right after they married, Grace and Vincent went on a trip to Europe, visiting locations in France, England, Scotland, and Wales. Grace was especially impressed by Stonehenge, a mysterious ancient structure made of enormous standing stones, weighing many tons each, that stand in a circle on Salisbury Plain in England.

The Hoppers settled in Poughkeepsie, New York, about a two-hour train ride from New York City. They owned a Model A Ford Roadster but apparently were too busy to clean it, because as Grace commented in *Grace Hopper: Navy Admiral and Computer Pioneer,* "That car never got washed."

Although they had a traditional, two-story home, Grace didn't plan on becoming a traditional housewife. Instead, she managed to continue studying for her Ph.D. at Yale by teaching at Vassar at the same time. Having an income from Vassar enabled Grace to continue her studies.

THE GREAT DEPRESSION

In the 1930s, America suffered through what is known as the Great Depression. Because of a crash in the stock market in 1929, the American economy suffered a crippling collapse. People went broke overnight and were desperate for work.

As an instructor at Vassar, Grace earned $800 a year. That may sound like an awfully small amount of money for a yearly salary, but money went a lot farther back then. For example, a loaf of bread cost eight cents, seeing a movie cost twenty-five cents, and you could buy a new car for less than $600.

When she began as an instructor at Vassar, Grace taught calculus, algebra, and trigonometry. Later, she added courses in analysis, theory of probability, and statistics. By the time she left Vassar in 1943, she was an associate professor.

A RARE ACHIEVEMENT

Grace completed her doctorate work at Yale in 1934 with a Ph.D. in mathematics. This was a rare achievement. During the years she worked on her doctorate there were only ten other students doing the same doctoral work at Yale, and only four of them were women, including Grace.

Women who studied under Grace and went on to have brilliant careers of their own praised Grace for being an outstanding and vibrant teacher. She was an inspiration to them and to many others who followed. However, this academic career was set aside when Grace's life was changed by the events of 1941.

3

Overcoming Obstacles

On December 7, 1941, Japan staged a surprise attack on the U.S. naval station at Pearl Harbor, Hawaii. The damage to the navy, as well as the loss of life, was a stunning outrage. Before that, the United States had not joined in the battles of World War II, but President Franklin D. Roosevelt and Congress quickly declared war on Japan and her allies, Germany and Italy.

Suddenly, America was plunged into action as it geared up to go to war. Everyone in the country was touched by feelings of grief, outrage, and patriotism. Grace first heard about the attack on Pearl Harbor while she was at home grading papers and listening to the radio.

After the Japanese attacked the U.S. naval base at Pearl Harbor, Hawaii, in 1941, the United States entered World War II. Many U.S. citizens joined the armed forces. Grace joined the United States Naval Reserve in 1943 and began her long career in the U.S. Navy.

SERVICE TO THE COUNTRY

Vincent Hopper and Grace's brother, Roger, both joined the U.S. Army Air Force. Her father worked for the Selective Service Board (which drafted men into the military services), her mother for the Ration Board (many basic supplies were rationed during the war, such as meat, sugar, and gasoline), and her sister, Mary, worked in a factory making fuses for bombs.

Grace's family had a long history of service to their country, going all the way back to the Revolutionary War. Grace's great-grandfather on her mother's side, Alexander Wilson Russell, was a rear admiral in the navy. She could recall how impressed she was with him even at the age of three. She described him in *Grace Hopper: Navy Admiral and Computer Pioneer*: "He was tall and straight, carried a black cane with a silver top on it, and had white muttonchop whiskers, which I had never seen before."

Grace was determined to find her own way to serve her country, but when she tried to join the navy, she found nothing but obstacles blocking her way. They said she was too old, although she was only thirty-four. They said she didn't meet the physical requirements. She stood five feet six inches and weighed only 105 pounds. They required her to weigh 121 pounds for that height. Their third argument was that her occupation as a mathematics professor was too important to the country and she was needed in the civilian sector. But none of this sat well with the unstoppable Grace, who had nothing else holding her back: Vincent and Grace had no children and had become separated. They eventually divorced in 1945. Vincent Hopper died that same year, and Grace never remarried.

JOINING THE WAVES

Serving in the navy became a challenge to overcome, and Grace Hopper never backed down from a challenge. She forced Vassar to give her a leave of absence from teaching by threatening to quit if she was not granted one. She managed to get a waiver to sidestep the age, height, and weight requirements. Grace was very resourceful.

Finally, in December 1943, Grace Hopper joined the U.S. Naval Reserve branch known as the WAVES (Women Accepted for Volunteer Emergency Service). This was how women had to join the navy at the time, since no women were allowed into the regular military.

At the time, about 30,000 to 40,000 other women had joined the WAVES. According to *Grace*

In 1942, the U.S. Navy adopted a policy of allowing women to enroll in the navy to fill clerical positions. A woman named Mildred McAfee was hired to supervise the WAVES (Women Accepted for Volunteer Emergency Service), as they were called.

Hopper: Navy Admiral and Computer Pioneer, when asked why she joined the navy, Grace said, "There was a war on! It was the only thing to do."

MIDSHIPMAN'S SCHOOL

Once she was accepted, Grace had to attend the Naval Reserve Midshipman's School for Women in Northampton, Massachusetts. She had to pass midshipman's school or be booted out of the navy.

She found herself surrounded by young women who were the age of the students she used to teach. They were housed in an old hotel, slept on bunk beds, and had to keep all their possessions in suitcases under their bunks.

There were tough everyday requirements. The bed sheets had to be tight enough so that a quarter would bounce off them. The women had to keep their shoes shined in any kind of weather. And, of course, they had training. Every day they took orientation courses. They had to learn all about the navy: its history, customs, and regulations. They had to learn to identify types of ships, submarines, and planes accurately and instantly. They had to undergo drills and physical education. Finally, they had reading assignments at night.

It was a tough education, but Grace graduated first in her class. Dr. Hopper became Lieutenant (junior grade) Hopper in June 1944. Upon becoming Lieutenant Hopper, Grace took flowers to her great-grandfather's grave. According to *Grace Hopper: Navy Admiral and*

Grace Hopper is pictured here on June 27, 1944, on the day of her graduation from Naval Reserve Midshipman's School for Women, where she graduated first in her class. Her education at the school helped Grace to excel in the navy, programming the earliest computers.

Computer Pioneer, Grace told him, "It's all right for females to be Navy officers."

Many of the women in the WAVES did clerical and secretarial work. Fortunately, the navy recognized that Grace Hopper had much more to offer.

4

The Navy Programmer

Grace's first assignment was with the Bureau of Ordnance Computation at the Cruft Laboratory at Harvard University. There she was introduced to the first digital computer, the Mark I. The Mark I was the brainchild of Dr. Howard Aiken, who conceived the device in 1937 and was able to develop it with help from Thomas Watson Sr., the founder of IBM, who later gave the machine to the navy. The Mark I completed its first successful test in January 1943.

"THE PRETTIEST GADGET"

However, on the day in 1944 when Grace first arrived, she knew nothing about a

Commander Howard Aiken, pictured here with Grace in 1946, was a tough boss to please. He demanded a lot from his employees and challenged them to do good work.

computing machine. Neither did anyone else outside of the top-secret project. She would be only the third person to program it, making her one of the first computer programmers in the United States.

Grace's first impression of the Mark I and her first experience with Commander Aiken were recorded in *Grace Hopper: Navy Admiral and Computer Pioneer*. When Grace first laid

The Mark I was an enormous machine, weighing five tons. Grace learned how to program the complicated machine and wrote a book explaining how to use it. This manual, called A Manual of Operation for the Automatic Sequence Controlled Calculator, was published by Harvard University in 1946.

eyes on the gigantic Mark I, she thought to herself, "Gee, that's the prettiest gadget I ever saw." She was quoted as saying the Mark I was "man's first attempt to build a machine that would assist the power of his brain rather than the strength of his arm."

Commander Aiken greeted Lieutenant Hopper with some rather frightening words: "Where the hell have you been?" She thought he was referring to the weekend she had just had off to visit her parents. It turned out that he'd been waiting for her to show up the entire time she was at midshipman's school. "I told them you didn't need that; we've got to get to work," Aiken said.

THE MARK I

The Mark I was fifty-one feet (about sixteen meters) long, eight feet (about two and one half meters) high, and five feet (about one and one half meters) deep. It had a four-horsepower motor. Instead of tiny, silent microchips, it used bulky mechanical relays that had to open and close to perform calculations. Imagine 3,300 of these clacking away! These days, we have devices that fit in the palm of a hand that are billions of times more powerful than that huge machine.

Dr. Howard Aiken was also a commander serving in the Naval Reserves. The navy had a profound interest in the development of the Mark I. It was used for various military purposes, such as calculating angles of new navy guns to take into account crosswinds, air density, and temperature. The navy also used it for calculating the area covered by a minesweeping detector as it was towed behind a ship, and performing the first top-secret mathematical simulation of the shock waves that might be produced by an atomic bomb. These were typical of the problems Grace worked on during her tenure at Cruft Laboratory.

TACKLING BINARY CODE

With no choice but to plunge right in, Grace was glad to have help from Robert Campbell and Richard Bloch, two naval officers who were of a lower rank than Grace. The machine understood only binary code, which is long lines of zeros and ones that comprise specific instructions to the computer. At the time, the only way to write this code required long hours of writing instructions that had to be input by punching holes on a continuous paper tape (or later on punched cards), which the machine would read. Each line of code was a separate step in a problem that the computer would solve.

In 1944, computers looked and worked much different than they do today. Here, Grace Hopper works on an early computer. This machine required manual operation, unlike modern computers.

A line of code was represented by how many holes could be punched across the width of the tape. There was space for twenty-four holes, or three groups of eight holes each. These three groups per line each represented one action for the computer to perform, or three actions per line of command. It was easy to make mistakes either by misreading the numbers or by punching the wrong holes.

THE FIRST COMPUTER PROGRAMMER

Grace Hopper was not the first woman to be a programmer. Ada Lovelace has the honor of being considered the first computer programmer because she devised a method for early calculating machines to repeat complex calculations automatically. She lived from 1815 to 1852 and was the daughter of the famous English poet Lord Byron. In 1843, she predicted such machines being used to produce graphics, compose music, and other scientific uses. The Pentagon named a software program "Ada" in her honor.

THE TEMPERAMENTAL MARK I

The Mark I could do calculations in one day that used to take six months to do by hand. Yet this machine, considered so amazing back then, could perform only three additions per second. The Mark I also had to be monitored twenty-four hours a day. Sometimes Grace and her crew would have to sleep at their desks in order to be close by in case something went wrong. And things often went wrong in those early days of experimentation and discovery.

The Mark I was so big that the crew sometimes had to get inside it to find the problem. When one of its thousands of relays failed, they would track it down by the sparks it emitted. Grace described one day when the Mark I kept shutting down every few seconds. A group of admirals chose that day to come by and see it in operation. Rather than let her staff be embarrassed, Grace leaned against the machine and secretly kept hitting the start button. The machine made all kinds of mistakes, but the admirals didn't know any better. They thought they were seeing a perfect machine in action!

Commander Aiken proved an invaluable mentor during Lieutenant Hopper's development as a programmer. She said of his leadership style in *Grace Hopper: Navy Admiral and Computer Pioneer*, "It was a challenge. You could make any mistake in the world once, but not twice."

One day, Aiken came into her office and told Grace that she was going to write a book. Despite her protests, she was ordered to write the book. It was called *A Manual of Operation for the Automatic Sequence Controlled Calculator*—possibly the first ever technical manual for a computer. It was published by Harvard University.

FINDING "BUGS"

There is a story that is strongly associated with Grace Hopper that comes up just about every time someone writes about her. The story says that she is responsible for coining two of the most commonly used words in the field of computers

The Mark II built upon the work that Grace and her crew did on the Mark I. Both machines were much less advanced than modern computers and were much larger. Their work aided in the development of computers as we know them today.

today: bug (a programming error) and debugging (to fix programming errors).

By 1945, the new generation of computer, the Mark II, had been built. According to *Grace Hopper: Navy Admiral and Computer Pioneer*, Grace said, "We had to build it in an awful rush—it was wartime—out of components we could get our hands on." This was during a very hot summer. Grace and her crew had to work in an

Grace Hopper is often credited with coining the term "bug" as it is commonly used to describe a computer problem. In truth, she did not come up with it, but she did use the term early on. After years of using the term "bug," an actual moth was found in the hardware of the Mark II. It was taped into the logbook to remember the amusing incident.

old building without air-conditioning, so they kept the windows open.

One hot day, the Mark II stopped. They tracked the problem down to a moth that had flown in through the open window, had gotten inside the computer, and had been killed by a relay opening and closing.

"We got a pair of tweezers. Very carefully, we took the moth out of the relay, put it in the logbook, and put scotch tape over it, " Grace explained. After that, whenever Commander Aiken came by and asked the team why they weren't making any progress, they would claim they were "debugging" the computer.

FICTIONAL BUGS VS. REAL BUGS

Grace, however, never claimed to have invented the term "bug," because in fact she hadn't. Dr. Peggy Aldrich Kidwell oversees the mathematics collections in the Smithsonian Institution's National Museum of American History in Washington, D.C., which contains some of Hopper's personal papers and logbooks. Dr. Kidwell wrote the article "Stalking the Elusive Computer Bug" in which she researched how the word "bug" came to be used for computer problems.

She showed that using the word "bug" to mean a problem with a piece of electrical hardware goes all the way back to Thomas Edison and to telegraph operators in the 1890s. It became a word that was used by engineers to include a flaw or a problem in any apparatus, plan, or system.

The engineers at IBM who worked on the Mark I in 1944 used "bug" in this way and may well have been the ones to pass it on to Grace Hopper and her crew.

The use of "bug" obviously appealed to Grace's quick wit and sense of humor. Among her papers are humorous drawings of imaginary "bugs" that Grace made while working on problems with the Mark I. She drew a "table worm" that looks like a piece of the paper tape used to program the computer. She drew a caterpillar-like creature, which she called the NRL (Naval Research Laboratory) bug and jokingly blamed it for sending the wrong data so that the machine got the wrong results. There was the "kitchie boo boo bug" that had to do with loose relays. On the same page, she drew a funny smiling face and labeled it "he who brings good data."

Obviously, Grace was able to have fun while doing serious mathematical work. Her drawings also reveal that she and her coworkers weren't looking for physical bugs and that they used the term loosely to refer to any small problem in either the hardware (the physical machine) or the software (the program).

Then came the day (circa 1947) when they found an actual moth in the relay. After years of joking about "bugs," you can imagine how funny it must have been to them to find the real thing! It's no wonder that they took it out with such care and taped it into the logbook.

However, Grace did help write glossaries of computer terms, and there's no doubt that she helped to popularize the use of the words "bug" and "debugging" in connection with computers. Today these are widely used words, especially in association with software. A bad piece of software is often referred to as buggy, and debugging is a vital part of completing any new program or releasing any piece of software.

5

A Computer Genius

While Grace was tracking down computer bugs, World War II was coming to an end. Germany surrendered on May 8, 1945, followed by the surrender of Japan on August 14, 1945. The long, terrible war was finally over.

In 1946, Grace was released from active duty. She wanted to transfer from the WAVES to service in the regular navy, which was allowing women to serve at that time. Once again she was told that she was too old. She was forty, and the cutoff age was thirty-eight.

In a typical bit of Grace Hopper humor, she explained in *Grace Hopper: Navy Admiral and Computer Pioneer*, "I always

When given the opportunity to continue her teaching job at Vassar, Grace turned it down in favor of staying on at the Harvard University Computation Lab, pictured here in 1946. It was at this lab that Grace began work on the Mark III.

explain to everybody it's better to be told you're too old when you're forty because then you go through the experience and it doesn't bother you again." She received the Naval Ordnance Development Award for her work with the Mark computer series (the Mark I and the Mark II) and was removed from active duty.

She could have gone back to her teaching job at Vassar, but computers were in her blood. They

Grace, here at her desk in the Harvard Computation Lab in 1947, helped to transform the world of computers. She had the foresight to realize how advanced computers could become and how important they could be to society.

were, as she put it, "more fun." She stayed on at the Harvard Computational Laboratory to help with the building of the Mark III.

COMPUTERS IN THE PRIVATE SECTOR

The Mark II was five times faster than the Mark I, the Mark III was fifty times faster than the Mark II, and the Mark IV would be even faster. Already, computers were improving in vast degrees of speed. Yet they still required mathematical skill and the time-consuming coding process to turn binary code into the necessary commands.

Grace worked at Harvard until 1949, when she took a bold step and went to work in the commercial sector. This was bold because, at the time, very few people other than Grace Hopper had a vision of what computers could become. Even IBM didn't think there would be a need for large numbers of computers or that we would eventually be using computers for business purposes. It looked as though everybody was going to settle for using punched cards forever.

FORESEEING THE FUTURE

Grace Hopper knew the importance of change and often spoke of it. An article in *Chips* magazine tells the story of Ginny Mullen, a retired navy commander, meeting Grace Hopper during a time when Grace worked on computers at the Pentagon. As the story goes, Grace would push a cart full of computer printouts from the computer workroom to her basement office. In that office, she had built something out of cardboard boxes, made to look like a television, with a picture taped to the area where the screen should be. She had labeled it "Personal Computer System." She told Mullen that "someday we would have the means of talking desk to desk, by computer."

Some of that inspiration may have come from her mentor, Howard Aiken, who envisioned a day when a computer would fill only a shoebox instead of an entire room. During Hopper's lifetime, she was able to see her predictions come true with the birth and development of personal desktop computers, the Internet, and e-mail.

THE NEXT WAVE OF COMPUTERS

But all of that lay far in the future at the time when Grace went to work for the Eckert-Mauchly Computer Corporation in Philadelphia. She was hired as senior mathematician.

J. Presper Eckert and John Mauchly had been developing their own electronic computers during

U.S. Army Major General Gladeon M. Barnes and Dr. John G. Brainerd discuss ENIAC with the cofounder of Eckert-Mauchly Computer Corporation Dr. John Mauchly (right). ENIAC was the first computer to run on electricity.

the war. The first was known as ENIAC (Electronic Numerical Integrator and Calculator). Like the Mark series, it was huge, more than 100 feet (about 30 meters) long and 10 feet (about 3 meters) high, contained more than 18,000 glass electronic vacuum tubes, and weighed more than 30 tons (27.2 metric tons). But instead of using mechanical devices such as levers, it used electrical pulses and had almost no moving parts.

Next they developed EDVAC (Electronic Discrete Variable Automatic Computer). It was faster and included other advances, such as being able to keep the instructions for a calculation in its memory instead of requiring external input.

When Grace went to work with Eckert and Mauchly, they were just completing BINAC (Binary Automatic Computer). One of Grace's jobs was to teach the people at Northrop Aircraft Corporation how to use it.

Eckert-Mauchly Computer Corporation was eventually bought by Remington Rand, which then merged into the Sperry Corporation, now known as UNISYS. Grace remained with them until 1967.

Many of Grace Hopper's peers did not believe that a computer could be programmed to understand English. Grace proved them wrong with the invention of COBOL (COmmon Business Oriented Language), which eventually became the standard programming language and is still in use today.

WORKING WITH UNIVAC I

The first attempt at a mass-produced, commercial computer took place in 1951. It was called UNIVAC I (Universal Automatic Computer). Instead of using punch cards, it used high-speed magnetic tape to record data. It was only fourteen and 1/2 feet (about 4 and 1/2 meters) long, 9 feet (about 3 meters) wide, and 7 and 1/2 feet (about 2 meters) tall—far smaller than earlier computers, and far, far faster.

There was a lot at stake in the development of UNIVAC I. Grace explained in *Grace Hopper: Navy Admiral and Computer Pioneer*, "Those were precarious days. We used to say that if UNIVAC I didn't work, we were going to throw it out one side of the factory which was a junkyard, and we were going to jump out the other side, which was a cemetery!"

The coding Grace was doing on these machines was based on the mathematical system known as octal. It uses a total of eight digits, starting with 0 and ending with 7. She had to teach herself to do all her math—adding, subtracting, multiplying, and dividing—in octal. She got very good at this, maybe a little too good. Pretty soon, she began to have trouble balancing her checkbook. Her brother, Roger, then a banker, went through her accounts and discovered that every once in a while, she'd use octal math instead of regular ten-digit math.

CREATING A NEW LANGUAGE

During this time, Grace became convinced that it would be possible to teach a computer to write its own programs. She knew there needed to be a way for ordinary people, rather than mathematicians who could do octal math, to tell a computer what to do. What was needed was a programming language that anybody could understand.

In 1952, Grace developed the A-0 System ("A" stands for algebraic, "0" was the first version). It was the first compiler. A compiler is a way to translate mathematical symbols that humans can read into machine code that a computer can understand. Grace had collected pieces of mathematical code, or routines, that were used over and over again in many different programs. Next, she gave each of these routines a call number. Then she could simply use the call number and that routine would be pulled from where it was stored on the magnetic tape and put into use.

As she described in *Grace Hopper: Navy Admiral and Computer Pioneer*, "All I had to do was to write down a set of call numbers, let the computer find them on the tape, bring them over and do the additions."

INSPIRATION FROM BASKETBALL

Grace used an unusual source of inspiration to solve one of the problems she had in creating the A-o compiler—her experience playing basketball. Back when Grace had been playing basketball, the rules allowed a woman to dribble only once, then not take another step, so to keep the ball moving forward she would have to throw a forward pass to another teammate. Then she would run to a new forward position and her teammate would throw the ball back to her.

According to *Grace Hopper: Navy Admiral and Computer Pioneer*, here's how she applied that to the compiler: "I tucked a little section down at the end of the memory which I called the 'neutral corner.' At the time I wanted to jump forward from the routine I was working on, I jumped to a spot in the 'neutral corner.' I then set up a flag for an operation which said, 'I've got a message for you.' This meant that each routine, as I processed it, had to look and see if it had a flag; if it did, it put a second jump from the neutral corner to the beginning of the routine."

It is difficult to convey just what a radical change in thinking and design the compiler was in the world of computers. It was the beginning of what we know as modern computer programs and was possibly Grace Hopper's greatest contribution to the development of computer software. It paved the way for everything that was to follow in the development of user-friendly computers. Every piece of software today, from spreadsheets to console games, relies on the use of compilers. Even the word "flag" is sometimes still used in computer programming to indicate something the computer is supposed to catch and do in response to the action of the user.

CREATING FLOW-MATIC

Grace didn't stop there. The A-0 evolved into the A-1 and the A-2 as she kept improving it. Yet it took Grace years to overcome industry skeptics and convince people of what her compiler could do.

Sometime around 1950, Charles H. Doersam Jr. was part of a small group of computer people, and Grace was the only woman in the group. In an article by Gordon R. Nagler for the National Academy of Engineering, Doersam related how Hopper created quite a stir by getting up and making this speech: "I've been coming to these meetings for some time now and listening to all of you men tell me about your fine hardware, and I think it's about time I tell you about my 'software.'"

Grace had the idea that computer programs could be written in English. She didn't see why the letters of the alphabet couldn't be translated into machine code the same as numbers and mathematical symbols.

In typically modest fashion, Grace claimed that no one thought of it before her because she was lazier than most people. She didn't want to spend all that time writing difficult code, she just wanted to get the work done. With that in mind, she developed the B-0 compiler ("B" standing for business), but it's probably better known for the name it acquired later, the FLOW-MATIC. It was specifically designed to handle business procedures such as payroll and billing.

It was a huge accomplishment when she was able to teach UNIVAC to read twenty written commands by 1956. The kind of words used by the FLOW-MATIC were add, multiply, subtract, divide, count, move, and replace.

Grace was so far ahead of her time she could see how the FLOW-MATIC would be adapted to other languages besides English. As usual, nobody wanted to believe her. They would say critical things, such as claiming that an American computer built in Philadelphia, Pennsylvania, couldn't understand French or German.

THE DEVELOPMENT OF COBOL

In the the mid-1950s, other companies were starting to follow suit by developing early

Here, Grace teaches a UNIVAC programming class in the 1960s. Grace first started working with UNIVAC in 1951 when she was working for the Eckert-Mauchly Corporation. After only five years of working with UNIVAC, Grace was able to teach the machine written commands.

programming languages such as FORTRAN (FORmula TRANslation), devised by IBM. None of them used English commands the way the FLOW-MATIC did. Furthermore, none of these languages were compatible with other machines. One type of programming language could only be used with one type of computer. There was no standard way to do things.

Finally, in 1959, a technical committee was formed that represented big business interests, the military, and the largest of the business machine manufacturers. They came up with a recommendation that had nothing to do with the programming languages developed by either IBM or UNIVAC. They called what they came up with COBOL (COmon Business Oriented Language). But there were a couple of problems. For one thing, their attempt to create a COBOL language didn't work. Second, IBM refused to accept it, and it would never get anywhere without agreement from IBM. Now the race was on for someone to come up with a version of COBOL that everyone would accept.

In 1960, Grace Hopper demonstrated a version of COBOL that would run on both UNIVAC and RCA computers. It was another two years before IBM finally accepted using COBOL as a standard language.

A European committee began to work with the American committee toward standardizing COBOL on a more global basis. Over the years, COBOL continued to grow and develop until it became the basis of nearly every computer program in the world. It was used to process large volumes of data and was utilized for such things as payroll, inventory, and accounting. The kind of basic words COBOL could process included run, move, get, add, multiply, divide, transfer, and stop. It is still widely in use today.

RECOGNITION FOR GRACE

Grace was acknowledged as one of the vital forces in creating COBOL. It was thanks to her vision and foresight that the language was written using easily understood English commands, in spite of unimaginative people telling her it couldn't be done.

This is one of the most significant changes in the history of computer evolution, and she won awards for it. In 1969, she was named the first-ever Computer Science Man of the Year by the Data Processing Management Association (although she was surely not a man!). In 1973, she became a Distinguished Fellow of the British Computer Society. By doing so, she became the first person from the United States and the first woman of any nationality to win this prestigious prize.

And there were many, many more awards earned during her lifetime. You'd think this was enough for most people, but Grace Hopper was just getting started.

6

Spreading Knowledge

In 1966, Grace received a letter from the navy reminding her that she had served in the Naval Reserves for twenty-three years. It also reminded her that she was sixty years old. Then she read on and realized that the letter was actually asking her to apply for retirement. Grace was saddened, but she retired from the reserves with the rank of commander. This retirement lasted for only seven months.

A new federal law gave the National Bureau of Standards the responsibility of overseeing the standardization of COBOL, and the man who had to do that job was Norman Ream, who had previously worked for the secretary of the navy. The navy was unable to develop a working payroll plan after 823 attempts. Norman Ream needed help, and he called for Commander Grace Hopper. It was supposed to be a temporary assignment of six months, but it lasted for almost twenty years.

"LIBERATING" THE FURNITURE

Grace was assigned a room in the Pentagon and was given a small staff to help her. What they didn't do was provide her with furnishings. Grace had to buy herself a coffeepot for her office. She and her staff came in at night and helped themselves to some furniture from other offices. When someone complained about the missing furniture, her defense was to say it was not bolted down.

Grace Hopper had a couple of other items that were unusual to find in a navy commander's office. She had a skull and crossbones pirate flag, a sure sign of her independent personality. And she had a clock that ran backward (counterclockwise). Grace kept this clock as a visual reminder to

Grace was promoted to the rank of captain in 1973. Even after her promotion, she was always willing and happy to discuss her work with others. Teaching was one of Grace's strong points, and she loved to spread her knowledge to others.

herself or anyone else that the words she hated to hear most were, "We've always done it that way." This clock was a prime example of a different but equally valid way of doing things. It seems odd only because we're not used to it. Elizabeth Dickason, writing about Grace Hopper for *Chips* magazine, said that Grace's message was this: Be innovative, open minded, and give people the freedom to try new things.

FACING A TOUGH AUDIENCE

Commander Hopper's position was director, Navy Programming Languages Group, Office of

Information Systems Planning and Development. Her title was quite a mouthful.

Here she was basically doing what she had been doing for years—finding ways to standardize the development of COBOL so that the system would work for all kinds of computers and programs, and to make sure that COBOL was used throughout the navy.

According to *Grace Hopper: Navy Admiral and Computer Pioneer*, Grace had to give a presentation to the secretary of the navy and other high-ranking officials. A navy captain (a higher rank than her rank as commander) was escorting her to the room where she'd have to give her speech. The captain said to her, "This is the first time a woman has ever given a presentation in that room." That didn't do much to put Grace at ease. Then he said, "This is the first time anyone below the rank of captain has given a presentation in that room." Grace remembered, "I was in fine shape by the time I got there."

She gave her speech, and afterward the secretary of the navy asked if there was anything she needed. Rather than being at all intimidated by whom she was talking to, Grace promptly asked for a larger staff and $20,000 to conduct a survey to find out what COBOL users needed.

He promised to do what he could and then "the room collapsed in one roar of laughter." Grace fled outside and asked the navy captain what on earth she had done. He said, "Don't you realize that no one ever asks for less than twenty million dollars in that room?"

In 1973, she was promoted to the rank of captain. This was also the year she was awarded the Legion of Merit, a special award created by Congress in 1942, given for the performance of outstanding services by military personnel.

GRACE, THE TEACHER

Grace remained in the navy for decades, but during that time she did far more than mathematical calculations and computer pro-gramming. One of the things she did best was teach, and she'd been doing that ever since she was a graduate student at Vassar.

No matter what else she was doing, whether she was working at a private company or for the navy, Grace traveled to teach and give lectures. She served as visiting lecturer or visiting associate professor at various engineering schools, including the ones at the University of Pennsylvania and George Washington University in Washington, D.C.

Grace didn't keep the money she received from her speaking engagements. Instead, she donated it—a total of $114,295—to the Navy Relief Society.

THE NANOSECOND

Grace was an excellent speaker who knew how to explain things in a way that was easy to understand. One of the examples for which she is especially well remembered was her explanation of the nanosecond.

As computers became faster and faster, Grace wrestled with understanding tinier and tinier units of time. Even though she knew the definition of a millisecond (one-thousandth of a second), it was still hard for her to understand it fully. Her frustration grew when she then tried to understand a microsecond (one-millionth of a second), a nanosecond (one-billionth of a second), and a picosecond (one-trillionth of a second).

Grace became so frustrated with trying to grasp these units that she made a call to some engineers and asked them to send her a nanosecond. She was probably just being funny, but the engineers took her seriously. Or at least they came up with a more or less serious way of answering her. They sent her a piece of wire that was 11.78 inches (about 30 centimeters) long. This piece of wire represented how far electricity could go through the wire in the amount of a nanosecond.

Grace was delighted. Next she asked for a piece of wire that would represent the length of a microsecond (a mere one-millionth of a second). This piece of wire was an entire coil that was 984 feet (about 300 meters) long!

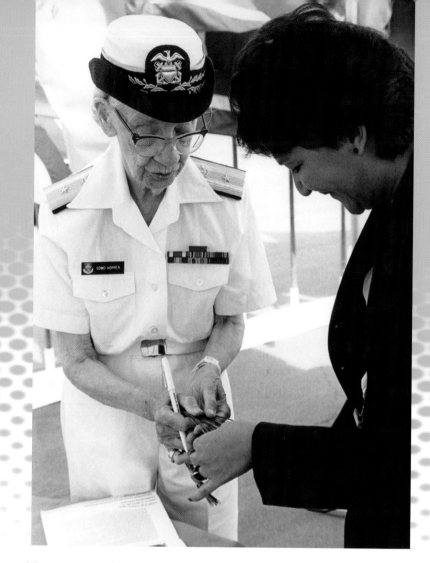

Many remember Grace for her interesting and memorable lecturing skills. When explaining the nanosecond, she often handed out pieces of wire that represented the distance electricity could travel in a nanosecond. This helped many people to understand complicated terms that are not so easily explained.

EXPLAINING NANOSECONDS

Grace explained in *Grace Hopper: Navy Admiral and Computer Pioneer,* "Sometimes I think that we should hang [a 984-foot coil of wire] on all programmers' desks or around their necks so they know exactly what they are throwing away when they throw away a microsecond."

Remember how the Mark I was thought to be so fast because it could do three operations per second? One operation can be getting a value out of memory, or storing another value in memory, or adding one value to another, and so on. Now we have memory chips that can do *billions* of operations per second, meaning more than one operation per nanosecond.

An admiral once asked Grace to explain why it took so long for a message to be sent by satellite. Grace pointed the nanosecond piece of wire toward space and explained to him that there were many nanoseconds between where they were and the satellite.

GIVING AWAY THE NANOSECOND

Grace would bring the nanosecond piece of wire and the microsecond coil of wire to the hundreds of lectures she gave, and they were always a big hit. Her lectures would be packed to overflowing, and afterward people would line up to receive one of Grace's nanoseconds, which she would hand out.

Linda Dunn, a systems manager, heard Grace speak in 1986. Here's how she described it in an interview: "She was an incredible speaker and had the audience eating out of her hand. The two sayings I always associate with Grace Hopper (and which I took to heart) were: 'It's easier to apologize later than to get permission first' and 'If it's not bolted down.' In government, quite a few of us followed both those philosophies. I went not knowing who she was and prepared to be bored. I walked out of there an admirer. She fairly radiated energy and enthusiasm. I was very, very disappointed not to get a nanosecond."

7

Taking Initiative

As Linda Dunn noted, another phrase for which Grace was extremely well known was, "It's easier to ask forgiveness than to get permission." She had a variety of stories she would tell to explain what she meant by this. One story was about a young navy lieutenant who served on a small ship. The navy thought the ship was too small to have a computer. The lieutenant brought his own computer with him and put all the ship's records into it. He was so efficient that when he left the captain had to buy the computer from him in order to keep the ship running properly.

In another version of the story, a sailor built a computer on a ship. This brought adventurous summers of her youth, a place she remembered fondly.

At this academy, she spoke about computers and visited two classes that taught COBOL programming. Both Grace and the staff of the academy were enthusiastic about the idea of establishing a computer center for the school. Grace used her many contacts within the industry to help make this happen. She turned to people at such large corporations as Wang, Digital Equipment Corporation, and 150 other businesses, convincing them to support the creation of the center.

About a year later, in November 1983, the academy was able to open the Grace Murray Hopper Center for Computer Learning. The governor of New Hampshire declared November 7 Captain Grace Murray Hopper Day.

KINDNESS TO OTHERS

In addition to being energetic and dedicated, Grace was a warm, generous woman. Ginny Mullen, a retired navy commander, told a story of

HOPPERISMS

Grace Hopper was known for her colorful quotes. Here are a few examples, compiled by Philip Scheiber for the *OCLC Newsletter* (Online Computer Library Center):

- "You manage things, you lead people."

- "We're flooding people with information. A human must turn information into intelligence or knowledge. We've tended to forget that no computer will ever ask a new question."

- "In pioneer days, they used oxen for heavy pulling, and when one ox couldn't budge a log, they didn't try to grow a larger ox. We shouldn't be trying for bigger computers, but for more systems of computers."

Grace's keen memory and thoughtfulness, which was published on the Navy *Chips* Web site.

It was a day when Mullen was relating how she had gotten into the navy. "I told her of having a godmother who had been a Radioman WAVE during

WWII and about the paper doll book I had been given." The next time Mullen ran into Hopper, Grace presented her with a book of WAVE and Marine Women paper dolls. It was the kind of gesture that made Grace Hopper a valued mentor to so many young people.

BECOMING A COMMODORE

The rank of captain was only a stop along the way to Grace's advancement in the navy. On December 15, 1983, she was promoted to the rank of commodore. At the time, Grace was seventy-six and she was considered too old to be eligible for promotion. Since it couldn't be done in the normal way, Representative Philip Crane introduced a bill into Congress to make it happen. He believed that it was time for Grace to be honored and recognized for her outstanding work. He became inspired to do this after seeing Grace on television doing an interview for the news show *60 Minutes*.

In 1983, a bill was passed into Congress to allow Grace her much deserved promotion to the rank of commodore. Many people took notice of Grace's incredible contributions, including the president of the United States, Ronald Reagan, pictured here congratulating Grace.

The bill was approved and Grace received her promotion by special presidential appointment from President Ronald Reagan.

BECOMING AN ADMIRAL

Two years later, in 1985, she was promoted once again to rear admiral. When she received that historic promotion, she was only the seventh

Grace Hopper (center) *attended the groundbreaking ceremony for the Grace Murray Hopper Service Center on September 27, 1985. The building is a 135,577 square-foot facility that contains a museum housing some of Grace's awards and honors.*

woman ever to become a rear admiral in the U.S. Navy. According *to Grace Hopper: Navy Admiral and Computer Pioneer*, she joked to some friends that her great-grandfather, the one who had been a rear admiral himself, "may rise from the dead" at the news.

It was also in September of 1985 that NARDAC (Navy Regional Data Automation Center) began building a new facility in San Diego, California (now known as the Naval

Grace was proud to wear her uniform. It was a symbol of her prestigious rank as rear admiral in the navy, a position that Grace worked hard to achieve.

Computer and Telecommunications Station). It was dedicated as the Grace Murray Hopper Service Center. The purpose of this center was to contain a data process center and to provide training facilities, teleconferencing and telecommunications capabilities, and the Grace Hopper Museum to display many of her awards, military decorations, and university degrees.

Grace loved to wear her uniform and would laugh over the way people misinterpreted who she was. She was mistaken for a flight attendant and once for a security guard. People were often surprised that someone of her age could still be in the navy. Time and again, Grace had been told she was too old or that she needed to retire.

THE NAVY MICRO CONFERENCE AND *CHIPS*

One of Admiral Hopper's other great areas of enthusiasm was the Navy Micro Conference, which began in 1982. Grace would give the keynote speech during the early years, as it grew from a small conference of about 400 people to a conference attended by thousands who came to exchange the latest information on computers. This conference is now known as Connecting Technology, and it takes place twice a year, once on the East Coast and once on the West Coast.

Along with giving the Micro Conference, NARDAC in Norfolk, Virginia, began publishing a newsletter called *Chips Ahoy*, which is now just called *Chips* magazine. Their founding motto is "Dedicated to Sharing Information, Technology and Experience."

Grace Hopper had a strong feeling about *Chips*. Diane Hamblen, who began editing the magazine in 1986, recalls with great humor her first meeting with the legendary Hopper in a memorial editorial she wrote for the April 1992 issue of *Chips*.

Hamblen decided to start her *Chips* career "with a bang" by interviewing Grace Hopper. She made the phone calls and a meeting was arranged for a Wednesday night at 9 PM, during one of the Micro Conferences. "Swell," Hamblen thought, "That's past my bedtime, and I was absolutely certain it was past lights out for a 70-year-old-plus, admiral or not."

At the appointed time, Hamblen showed up with her tape recorder, spare tapes, pen and paper, and list of questions. Exactly at nine o'clock, Admiral Hopper showed up at the lobby of the hotel. She walked up to Hamblen, shook her hand and said, "So you're the new *Chips* editor. What makes you think you can do the job?"

From this daunting start, Hamblen began the interview, ". . . But it sure established who controlled who. We talked; I asked my questions. She talked; I changed tapes. She talked some more; I changed tapes again. I ran out of tape. She was winding up; I was winding down."

Hamblen admits that by 10:45 it was way past her bedtime and she was sagging, but by that time, Hopper had gathered an audience of interested listeners. At midnight, she said, "I tottered to my car, leaving her still holding court with her fan club."

The next morning, Hamblen was at work when her boss rushed up in a panic. "Admiral Hopper wants to see you. You left last night before she was finished."

That is how Hamblen found herself towed around the convention center behind the diminutive admiral, with Hopper "all the while lecturing me on what she expected from *Chips*."

A FINAL RETIREMENT

On August 14, 1986, at the age of seventy-nine, Grace Hopper retired from the navy for the final time. She asked to have her retirement ceremony

Grace Hopper's retirement ceremony took place on the USS Constitution, *a famous ship that was also known as Old Ironsides for its remarkable strength despite its age. Many people attended the gathering to show respect for Grace and her impressive naval career.*

take place on the deck of a famous ship, the USS *Constitution*, also known as Old Ironsides. She must have felt something in common with the ship: It was the oldest commissioned warship still in use, and when she retired she was the oldest commissioned officer on active duty.

It was a huge ceremony with full honors attended by about 300 people: friends, navy officials, dignitaries, people who had worked with her in World War II, and members of her family.

The secretary of the navy, John F. Lehman Jr., gave her the Distinguished Service Medal of the Department of Defense, which he pinned onto her uniform. It is the Defense Department's second-highest honor that can be awarded.

As reported by Richard Pearson for the *Washington Post*, on January 4, 1992, Lehman told this joke: "I'm reminded of that famous story by P. T. Barnum. About the turn of the century, his principle attraction, the human cannonball, came to P. T. Barnum and said, 'Mr. Barnum, I just can't take it any longer. Two performances a day and four on weekends are just too much. I'm quitting.' Barnum said, 'You can't possibly quit. Where will I find someone else of your caliber?'"

He also said of Grace: "She's challenged at every turn the dictates of mindless bureaucracy." He also recalled, "[Once Hopper] gave me a stern lecture on computers. It was the roughest wire brushing I've had since I got this job."

Aboard the USS Constitution, Grace salutes the crew members at her retirement ceremony. After forty-three years of service, Grace was the oldest officer on active duty in the U.S. Navy.

There were more speeches made, a printed citation was handed out, a navy band played patriotic songs, sailors cheered, and Grace was given forty-three long-stemmed roses to signify her forty-three years of service to the navy.

This time, Admiral Hopper had truly retired, right? Not exactly.

8

The Making of a Legend

Retiring didn't mean slowing down. Though she was now officially retired from the navy, Grace Hopper remained active. She went to work for Digital Equipment Corporation (DEC) as a senior consultant. For DEC, Grace represented the organization at industry events, gave presentations on advanced computing concepts and the importance of information and data, and worked with schools.

For the next four years or so, she did lecture tours around the country to colleges, universities, and engineering forums. She continued to receive awards. In September 1991, when Grace was eighty-four, she received

AWARDS NAMED FOR DR. HOPPER

In addition to the huge number of awards Dr. Hopper received during her life, there are numerous awards that have been named in her honor. Here are some of them:

- The Grace Murray Hopper Award for Outstanding Young Scientist: A prestigious award given by the Association for Computing Machinery.

- The Grace Hopper Award for Computing and Grace Hopper Scholarships: This award is given by the Grace Hopper Celebration of Women in Computing, an annual technical conference.

- The Grace Hopper Government Technology Leadership Awards (also known as The Gracies): These are given out by the United States General Services Administration.

- The Grace Hopper Memorial Award: This is a scholarship in computer science given by Bowling Green State University in Ohio.

The Grace Hopper Lecture Series: This is run each year by the University of Pennsylvania's School of Engineering and Applied Science. It is intended to serve the dual purpose of recognizing successful women in engineering and inspiring students to achieve at the highest level.

Rear Admiral Grace Hopper Cup: This prize is awarded by the Arizona Civil Air Patrol to the "Arizona launch-team member who demonstrates innovative leadership solutions and the ability to think 'outside the box.'"

the National Medal of Technology. This is the United States's highest honor in engineering and technology, and Grace Hopper was the first woman individually recognized with the award.

In fact, at the end of her life she had two apartments—one that she lived in, and one that was overflowing with her papers and memorabilia. One room alone was filled entirely with plaques she had received over the decades.

Grace poses in her office in Washington, D.C., in 1984. When she began working with computers, they were massive, slow machines. During her lifetime she was able to see the evolution of computers, due in large part to her efforts.

A VISIONARY OUTLOOK

From beginning to end, Grace was a visionary. She saw the potential for computers to do such things as track the life cycle of crop-eating locusts, track waves at the bottom of the ocean, run all the electrical systems in a house, handle family bookkeeping and accounts, manage water reserves to guarantee a fair distribution of water, and perform weather prediction on a global scale.

She even foresaw more radical changes in computers when they might be powered by bursts of light instead of electricity.

Grace was especially concerned about weather prediction and water usage. She looked ahead to the importance of how climate changes would affect the planet, and she anticipated how the continuously increasing population will find itself competing more and more for limited water sources.

As far back as 1971, Grace talked about one of the goals she had had since childhood. She wanted to go to the stars. According to *Grace Hopper: Navy Admiral and Computer Pioneer*, Grace said, "Some day many millions of years from now the sun will go nova—that is, blow up, and the universe with it. We must get off the planet Earth and find another place for the human race to live. The present is not too soon to start on this quest. The computer will be man's greatest tool in attaining this new home for mankind." There is no doubt that we couldn't design our spacecraft and carry out our current space missions without the use of advanced computers, just as she foresaw.

A LONG LIFE

Going to the stars was a dream Grace wasn't able to fulfill, along with one other wish—she wanted to live to be ninety-four so she could celebrate the arrival of the new millennium in 2000. She figured that would be the greatest of all New Year's Eve parties.

Sadly, she didn't live to usher in the year 2000. Grace Hopper died in her sleep after a heart attack on New Year's Day, January 1, 1992. She was eighty-six years old.

Admiral Hopper was buried with full military honors at Arlington National Cemetery in Virginia. This historic cemetery has served as a burial ground since 1864 for soldiers and others who have served in the military or have performed special service in connection with the military. Hopper is well qualified to have her resting place there.

The funeral took place on Tuesday, January 7, 1992. The service began with a navy band playing a hymn. A navy color guard escorted the admiral's casket into the memorial chapel at Fort Myer, where the admiral's flag was draped in black and placed at the front. The navy chaplain read from the Old Testament of the Bible.

The chaplain spoke of Hopper's numerous achievements, of her great love for the navy, and her devotion to serving her country. He spoke of how she encouraged young people to reexamine how things were done to improve them instead of doing things out of habit. When Hopper would leave a meeting, the chaplain recounted, she would often leave with the words, "Fair winds and following seas." An organist played several versions of the beautiful eighteenth-century hymn "Amazing Grace."

The color guard accompanied the casket to the cemetery. The navy band walked in front, while family and friends walked behind it. At the graveside, the chaplain read another passage from Scripture. The color guard and band came to attention during a military salute, both an eleven-gun salute from a howitzer battery, which is a type of cannon (for her status as an admiral), and a twenty-one-gun salute for a fallen member of the armed forces.

GRACE'S LEGACY

Grace's legacy lives on in the many contributions she made to computer technology and programs. She was the inspiration for the Grace Hopper Celebration of Women in Computing, which is an annual conference designed to engage and inform women who have careers in computers.

THE USS *HOPPER* DDG 70

The USS *Hopper* is an Arleigh Burke-Class guided missile destroyer. It was first put into service on January 6, 1996. The USS *Hopper* is 465.9 feet (142 meters) long and can travel at more than 31 knots (approximately 35.7 miles per hour, or 57.1 kilometers per hour). It carries a crew of 325. The ship is packed with weapons, electronic warfare systems, and various types of sensors such as radar and sonar.

The ship's motto is "Aude et Effice," which is Latin for "Dare and Do." This motto was taken as a direct quote from words often used by Rear Admiral Hopper. According to the navy's Web site, "The

In addition to the Grace Murray Hopper Service Center and the Grace Murray Hopper Center for Computer Learning, there is also the USS *Hopper*, a navy ship named in her honor.

phrase captures the spirit of RADM Hopper in her quest for pushing the limits of conventional thinking and looking beyond the norm for innovative solutions and approaches to problem solving."

Or, as Admiral Hopper liked to say, "A ship in port is safe, but that is not what ships are built for."

The USS Hopper *was named in Grace's honor.*

WORDS OF ADVICE

Though Grace would undoubtedly have been impressed by her namesake ship, bristling with hardware and computers, there is no doubt that the legacy she valued the most was connecting to younger people, especially those between the ages of seventeen and twenty. Elizabeth Dickason reported in an article in the April 1992 issue of *Chips* that Grace said, "Working with the youth is the most important job I've done. It's also the most rewarding."

In *Grace Hopper: Navy Admiral and Computer Pioneer*, Hopper advised young people not to waste energy coming up with a life plan, but to be prepared to "grab every opportunity that comes down the pike." To do that, she recommended, "No smoking, no alcohol, and no drugs. Never risk anything that will damage your brain. If you are going to enjoy music, pictures, books, anything, you need your mind at its freshest, not damaged by alcohol or drugs. Besides which, the only way you're going to earn a living is using your head."

Grace Hopper lived a long and fruitful life. She is remembered as a computer pioneer, a mathematics whiz, and an excellent teacher. Her contributions to the field of computer science will always be remembered.

Grace was quoted in the April 1985 issue of the *Worthington Descendants Newsletter* as saying, "I like the world of today much better than that a half-century ago. Today the challenges are greater. I like our young people, they know more, they question more, and they learn more. They are the greatest asset this country has."

Though Grace Hopper is gone, her spirit and accomplishments have changed our world. The best way to honor her memory is to live up to her motto: Dare and Do.

TIMELINE

1906 Grace Murray Hopper is born Grace Brewster Murray on December 9 in New York City.

1924 Grace is accepted into and begins studies at Vassar College.

1928 Grace graduates from Vassar with a bachelor of arts degree in mathematics and physics. She begins her graduate studies at Yale University.

1930 On June 15, the twenty-three-year-old Grace Murray marries Vincent Foster Hopper.

1934 Grace receives a Ph.D. in mathematics from Yale University. During these years, she works on her doctorate, and she is one of only four women in the program.

1943 Grace joins the WAVES, a branch of the U.S. Naval Reserve.

1944 In June, Grace is promoted to the rank of lieutenant (junior grade).

1946 Grace is released from active duty. She hopes to transfer into the regular navy, but she is forty years old and the cutoff age for enrollment in the navy is thirty-eight.

1952	Grace develops the first computer compiler, called the A-o System.
1969	Grace is the first person named Computer Science Man of the Year by the Data Processing Management Association.
1973	Grace is promoted to the rank of captain. She is also awarded the Legion of Merit that year by Congress for her outstanding service to the military.
1985	Grace is promoted to rear admiral. At the time, she is only the seventh woman ever to become a rear admiral in the U.S. Navy.
1986	On August 14, at the age of seventy-nine, Grace Hopper retires from the navy for the final time. A retirement ceremony takes place on the USS *Constitution*, a boat nicknamed Old Ironsides.
1991	Grace receives the National Medal of Technology—the United States's highest honor in engineering and technology. Grace is the first woman individually recognized with the award.
1992	On New Year's Day, Grace suffers a heart attack in her sleep and passes away. She is eighty-six years old.

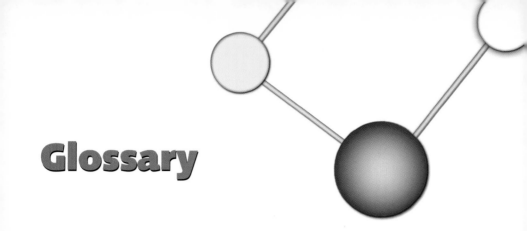

Glossary

algebra A branch of mathematics in which the operations and procedures of addition and multiplication are applied to variables as well as to specific numbers.

binary Consisting of two parts or components; also a mathematical system that uses just two numbers, zero and one, to represent all possible values.

bit Short for binary digit, the smallest unit of information a computer can process. Bits can have the values 1 (on) or 0 (off).

botany The branch of biological science that deals with the classification and study of plants.

bug A flaw or a problem in a machine, plan, or system.

byte A unit of binary code consisting of eight bits that can be used to represent a single letter or number.

calculus The branch of mathematics used in physics to calculate rates of change and the area and volume of spaces that change.

compiler A computer program that converts other programs from their programming language version into a form understandable by computers (called binary code).

data Facts, statistics, or other information.

debug, debugging To remove the flaws or errors from a machine, program, plan, or system.

digital Computer technology that uses numerical digits to process information.

geology The study of the physical structure, composition, and development of the earth or of rocks.

grant The giving of money for a specific purpose, such as education.

hymn A devotional song that is sung at a religious service.

knot The speed at which a ship can travel a nautical mile (about 1.5 miles) in an hour.

octal A mathematical system that uses eight numbers, beginning with 0 and ending with 7, to represent all possible values.

ordnance Cannon, artillery, and all kinds of military weapons, equipment, and ammunition.

patriotism A feeling of pride, love, and devotion to one's country.

physics The science that deals with matter and energy, their properties, and their interactions.

physiology The science that deals with the processes and functions of living organisms and their cells, tissues, and parts.

program A set of steps written in a code under-standable by machines that tells a computer how to solve a problem or perform an action.

trigonometry The branch of mathematics that deals with the relations between the sides and angles of triangles.

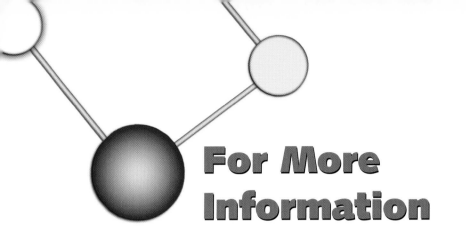

For More Information

Institute for Women and Technology
1501 Page Mill Road, MS 1105
Palo Alto, CA 94304
(650) 236-4756
Web site: http://www.iwt.org

Math/Science Network
Mills College
5000 MacArthur Boulevard
Oakland, CA 94613-1301
(510) 430-2222
Web site: http://www.expandingyourhorizons.org

The National Women's Hall of Fame
76 Fall Street
P.O. Box 335
Seneca Falls, NY 13148
(315) 568-8060
Web site: http://www.greatwomen.org

Society of Women Engineers
Executive Offices & Member Service Center
230 E Ohio Street, Suite 400
Chicago, IL 60611-3265
(312) 596-5223
Web site: http://www.swe.org

Women's International Center
P.O. Box 880736
San Diego, CA 92168-0736
(619) 295-6446
Web site: http://www.wic.org

WEB SITES

Due to the changing nature of Internet links, the Rosen Publishing Group, Inc., has developed an online list of Web sites related to the subject of this book. This site is updated regularly. Please use this link to access the list:

http://www.rosenlinks.com/whfms/ghop/

For Further Reading

Casey, Susan. *Women Invent: Two Centuries of Discoveries That Have Shaped Our World.* Chicago, IL: Chicago Review Press, 1997.

Hopper, Grace Murray, and Steven L. Mandell. *Understanding Computers.* St. Paul, MN: West Publishing Company, College & School Division, 1990.

Kass-Simon, G., and Patricia Farnes, eds. *Women of Science: Righting the Record.* Bloomington, IN: Indiana University Press, 1993.

Schneider, Carl J., and Dorothy Schneider. *Grace Murray Hopper: Working to Create the Future.* Las Cruces, NM: Sofwest Press, 1998.

GRACE HOPPER

Thimmesh, Catherine. *Girls Think of Everything: Stories of Ingenious Inventions by Women.* New York: Houghton Mifflin, 2000.

Whitelaw, Nancy. *Grace Hopper: Programming Pioneer.* New York: Scientific Books for Young Readers, 1995.

Williams, Kathleen Broome. *Improbable Warriors: Women Scientists and the U.S. Navy in World War II.* Annapolis, MD: Naval Institute Press, 2001.

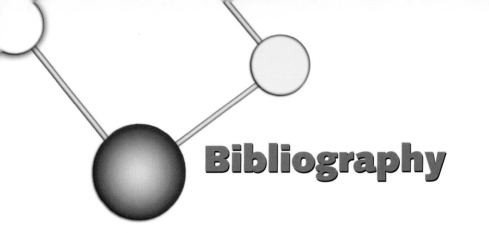

Bibliography

"A Living Lady Worthington Descendants Subscriber."
Worthington Descendants Newsletter, Vol. 1, No. 4,
April 1985.

Billings, Charlene W. *Grace Hopper: Navy Admiral
and Computer Pioneer*. Hillside, NJ: Enlsow
Publishers, 1989.

Dickason, Elizabeth. "Remembering Grace Murray
Hopper: A Legend in Her Own Time." *Chips*,
April 1992.

Hamblen, Diane. "Memorial Editorial." *Chips*, April 1992.

Kidwell, Peggy Aldrich. "Stalking the Elusive Computer
Bug." *IEEE Annals of the History of Computing*, Vol.
20, No. 4, 1998.

Mullen, Ginny. "I Remember." *Chips* Web site. Retrieved
May 2002 (http://www.norfolk.navy.mil/chips/
grace_hopper/ginny.htm).

Nagler, Gordon R. The National Academy of
Engineering. "Memorial Tributes: National Academy
of Engineering." Volume 6, 1993.

Index

ABOUT THE AUTHOR

Christy Marx has written for television, film, animation, computer games, and comic books. Among the shows she has written for are *Babylon 5*, *The Twilight Zone*, *He-Man*, *Stargate: Infinity*, *X-Men: Evolution*, *Beast Wars*, *ReBoot*, *G. I. Joe*, and *Jem and the Holograms*. She has designed both PC and console games, and has written for online role-playing games. Christy lives in California with her lifemate and a horde of cats. Visit her Web site at http://www.christymarx.com.

PHOTO CREDITS

Cover and background image © Digital Vision/Getty Images; cover inset, pp. 50, 99 © AP/Wide World Photos; p. 10 © Library of Congress; pp. 16, 17 © Vassar College Libraries, Archives and Special Collections Department; pp. 19, 41 courtesy of the U.S. Naval Historical Center; p. 24 © Scott Swanson Collection/ Archive Photos; p. 27 © Culver Pictures; pp. 29, 32, 40, 46, 47 courtesy of Grace Murray Hopper Collection, Archives Center, National Museum of American History, Smithsonian; p. 33 courtesy of IBM Corporate Archives; p. 36 © Bettmann/Corbis; p. 37 © Hulton/Archive; p. 52 courtesy of Smithsonian Institution Photo No. 83-14874; p. 59 courtesy of Smithsonian Institution Photo No. 83-14875; p. 65 courtesy of David C. MacLean/U.S. Naval Historical Center; pp. 70, 80 courtesy of Michael Flynn/U.S. Naval Historical Center; pp. 75, 79, 81, 97 courtesy of Defense Visual Information Center; p. 85 courtesy of U.S. Navy photo; p. 87 © AP/ Wide World Photos; p. 92 © Cynthia Johnson/Timepix.

DESIGN AND LAYOUT

Evelyn Horovicz

EDITOR

Eliza Berkowitz